Key Milestones for Growing Up Fast

Essential Insights for Tracking and Supporting Your Baby's Development for the first 6 months

Adegboye S. Aduragbemi

INTRODUCTION

Greetings from the beautiful realm of parenthood, where you will discover new things and enjoy surprises every day as you watch your child develop and flourish. It is expected to have concerns about your baby's development and well-being during the first few months of their existence because they are undergoing rapid growth and change.

We are excited to offer a thorough guide to understanding and assisting your baby's growth throughout the crucial time between two and six months of age in this book. We can answer your most urgent inquiries and provide insightful information on your child's growth and development as they explore their surroundings and hit significant milestones.

Every chapter in this book delves into a different area of your baby's development, from physical milestones like rolling over and gripping objects to cognitive leaps in awareness and social relationships. Our goal is to provide you with the knowledge and self-assurance you need to traverse this exciting period of motherhood with ease and assurance by compiling frequently asked questions (FAQs) and expert responses.

Remind yourself that you are your growing baby's best support system and advocate as you embark on this exciting journey of discovery together. As you nurture and mentor your child through their early milestones, let's celebrate the wonder of infancy and treasure every second of this unique time.

Cheers to the incredible road ahead and the innumerable pleasures of witnessing your child grow and thrive!

Chapter One

The process of physical development in infants

What is the expected growth rate for my kid in the second to sixth month?

Babies usually flourish at this time. Infants typically gain 1.5 to 2 pounds (0.7 to 0.9 kilograms) and grow 1 inch (2.5 centimetres) in length each month.

When should my child begin to hold their head up consistently?

Most babies can keep their heads up steadily when supported while sitting by the time they are 2 to 3 months old, and by the time they are 4 to 6 months old, they can frequently hold their heads up on their own when lying on their stomachs.

When will my infant begin to turn over?

Between the ages of 4 and 6 months, babies usually start rolling over from front to back and vice versa. When you give your infant supervised tummy time, you're encouraging their motor development.

When will my infant begin to grasp and reach for things?

Many babies start reaching for and batting at items when they are 3 or 4 months old. At five or six months old, babies might begin to hold things in their hands and use their senses to investigate them.

What is the recommended weight growth for my baby between the second and sixth months?

Babies typically gain 1.5 to 2 pounds (0.7 to 0.9 kg) every month during this time. Individual development rates, however, can differ, so it's essential to track your baby's growth trajectory instead of concentrating just on numbers.

How much longer should my infant get during this time?

Babies usually gain one inch (or 2.5 cm) in length per month between the ages of two and six months. Once more, while individual growth rates may differ, consistent growth is typically a sign of general health and progress.

How can I monitor my infant's growth and development during this phase?

By making regular well-child visits with your paediatrician, you can monitor the growth and development of your infant. Your baby's weight, length, and head circumference will be measured, and your paediatrician will evaluate their developmental milestones at these appointments.

What are some indicators that my kid is developing and doing well during this time?

Consistent weight gain, growing longer, reaching developmental milestones, and exhibiting attentiveness, responsiveness, and curiosity about their environment indicate your kid is healthy and developing.

What kinds of things can affect my baby's growth at this point?

Several factors can affect your baby's growth during the second to sixth month of pregnancy, including genetics, nutrition, general health, and environmental influences. Healthy growth and development can be supported by providing your kid with a safe and nurturing environment, enough food, and routine medical checks.

To promote my baby's growth and development, how often should I feed them?

Breastfed infants usually feed whenever they feel like it, which could mean that they feed every two to three hours or more frequently. An infant fed by formula may have a similar feeding pattern, but your baby's specific needs will determine how often and how much they are fed.

Should I be worried if my baby's growth rate slows down now?

While some variation in growth rates is typical, a noticeable or protracted slowing in growth may call for additional testing by your paediatrician. Your baby's growth trajectory may be impacted by illness, feeding issues, or underlying medical concerns, among other things.

What can I do at home to encourage my baby's healthy development and growth?

You can promote your baby's healthy growth and development by offering balanced food, participating in interactive play and sensory experiences, encouraging regular sleep and rest, and creating a secure and exciting environment for exploration and movement.

What are some telltale signs that my child receives enough nutrition to thrive?

Constant weight gain, comfort after feedings, constant diaper output (wet and dirty diapers), and meeting developmental milestones on time are indicators that your baby is receiving enough nutrition for healthy growth.

When will my child be able to balance on their legs?

By the time they are three or four months old, many newborns can support their weight on their legs. It is frequently observed when engaging in activities like standing with support or bouncing on a caregiver's lap.

How can I support my infant's motor skills development at this stage?

By giving your baby opportunities for supervised tummy time, letting them explore various textures and surfaces, and providing toys that encourage reaching, gripping, and kicking, you may support the development of your baby's motor abilities.

When will my child begin to show signs of hand-eye coordination?

The development of hand-eye coordination usually starts between the ages of three and six months. As your baby's motor skills develop, you can notice that they are reaching for objects with greater purpose and accuracy during this period.

What are some telltale signals that my child is prepared to sit up on their own?

Your baby will be able to hold their head steady without assistance, have adequate upper body control, and show interest in sitting up and reaching for items when ready to start sitting up on their own.

Should I be worried if my child is not meeting developmental milestones by now?

Although it's typical for babies to complete developmental milestones at varying rates, it's crucial to communicate any worries about your baby's physical development, such as delayed motor skills or mobility difficulties, with your paediatrician to receive additional assessment and advice.

How can I create a home environment conducive to my baby's physical development?

By ensuring your baby has lots of opportunities for supervised play and exploration, providing toys and activities that promote movement and engagement, and creating a safe and stimulating area where they can move around freely, you can make an environment that supports their physical development.

When will my child begin to demonstrate hand dominance?

Between six and twelve months, hand dominance, or a preference for using one hand over the other, may begin to show symptoms. Nonetheless, during the first year of life, it's normal for babies to explore and utilize both hands equally.

How can I ensure the infant I breastfeed gets enough nourishment for healthy growth?

Breastfeed your baby whenever you feel like it, and make sure you latch on to it and feed it properly to ensure it gets enough nutrients. It would be best to eat a healthy diet because your nutrition directly impacts the quality of your breast milk.

When will my baby's growth rate slow after accelerating so much in the first several months?

After the first few months, a baby's growth rates usually level off, resulting in a progressive drop in weight gain and an increase in the intervals between growth spurts. This slowing is natural as your baby's growth becomes more consistent and predictable.

Can I use milestones or growth charts to monitor my baby's development and growth?

Yes, clinicians frequently use growth charts to monitor a baby's growth over time. Healthcare professionals can track growth patterns and spot any possible concerns by comparing your baby's measures (weight, length, and head circumference) to standardized growth curves using these charts.

What part does sleep play in my baby's development during this growth and maturation period?

Since sleep is when growth hormone is predominantly secreted, getting enough sleep is essential for your baby's growth and development. Establish a regular bedtime routine, provide a peaceful sleeping environment, and react quickly to your baby's sleep cues to promote healthy sleep habits.

How can I encourage my baby to build healthy bones at this stage?

Ensure your infant gets enough calcium and vitamin D from breast milk, formula, or supplements as directed by your paediatrician to support healthy bone development. Encourage weight-bearing practices like supported sitting and tummy time as well.

What should I do if my baby's growth isn't as quick as I would like?

Talk to your paediatrician about any worries regarding your child's growth. To promote healthy growth and development, your doctor can evaluate your baby's growth patterns, treat any underlying conditions, and offer advice on diet, feeding, and general care.

Is it typical for my child to experience growth spurts at this time, and if so, how can I spot them?

Growth spurts are common in infants during the first year of life. Fussiness, increased appetite, and frequent feedings might indicate a growth spurt. Usually lasting a few days to a week, these bursts are followed by a rest and adjustment phase.

Chapter Two

Development of communication and verbal skills in infants

During this phase, how can I support my infant's language development?

Talking, singing, and reading aloud to your infant are all forms of frequent verbal connection. As your baby coos, babbles, or makes other vocalizations, respond to them and teach essential words and sounds while engaging in daily activities.

When is a baby supposed to start chattering and cooing?

Babbling starts between 4 and 6 months, after which babies usually start cooing around 2 or 3 months. These vocalizations are a crucial stage before language acquisition.

During this phase, how can I support my infant's language development?

Communicate with your infant verbally regularly. Talk to them about things, feelings, and activities as the day progresses. React enthusiastically to their coos and babbles, making sounds similar to them and promoting back-and-forth "conversations."

When will my child begin to react when their name is called?

Many babies learn to know and react to their name when it is said by the time they are 4 to 6 months old. Use it often to help your baby form a pleasant and engaging relationship with their name.

How can I introduce activities that are rich in language to my infant?

Starting from the time of birth, read essential stories and picture books to your infant. Introduce new words and sounds to your infant by playing games like peekaboo, singing nursery rhymes, and playing music.

If my six-month-old infant is not babbling, should I be worried?

Although each baby grows at their rate, it could be worth talking to your paediatrician if your child isn't babbling or making vocalizations by the time they are six months old. They can evaluate your baby's hearing and general development to ensure no underlying issues.

How can I help my infant with their receptive language skills or language understanding at this stage?

When conversing with your infant, speak in plain, straightforward terms and give them opportunities to react to hints and commands in voice. To assist your infant in understanding English, point out recognizable items, body parts, and people in their surroundings.

When is my infant likely to start mimicking words and sounds?

Babies can start mimicking noises and rudimentary sentences as early as 4 to 6 months, depending on the child. Promote imitation by complimenting your baby's attempts at communication and mimicking the noises and words they create.

How does nonverbal communication affect the linguistic development of my infant?

Early language development heavily relies on nonverbal cues such as body language, gestures, and facial expressions. Observe your infant's nonverbal clues and react accordingly to help lay the groundwork for future successful communication.

How can I help my infant develop early literacy skills at this time?

Provide interactive toys and board books appropriate for the child's age to promote exploration and manipulation. To foster in your baby a love of books and reading, create a comfortable reading space and incorporate reading into your everyday routine.

What are some indicators that my child's language development is advancing?

Increased vocalizations, imitation efforts, familiar word and sound identification, and responsiveness to verbal cues and interactions indicate language development advancement.

When will my infant begin to distinguish between sounds and voices they know?

Babies may start to favour the voices of people they know, particularly their caregivers, by the time they are two or three months old. They can swivel their heads or exhibit other recognition-related behaviours when they hear a familiar voice.

What are some tactics for encouraging play-based early language development?

Take part in interactive play activities with your baby, where you can sing, talk, and make sounds. They use toys with textured surfaces or varied noises to excite their senses and promote exploration.

Should I tell my infant about my everyday activities even though they cannot yet understand?

Yes, telling your infant about your everyday activities will assist them in getting familiar with language rhythms and patterns. It offers connecting and conversation opportunities before kids can comprehend your words.

What are "serve and return" exchanges, and what role do they play in language acquisition?

In "serve and return" interactions, you react appropriately and promptly to your baby's vocalizations, gestures, or expressions. These exchanges build the relationship between you and your child and lay the groundwork for future communication abilities.

When is the right time to start communicating with my kid using signs and gestures?

Simple signals and gestures, such as kisses or waving bye-bye, can be used as early as six months. These gestures can facilitate the transition from your baby's early attempts at communicating to their capacity to utilize words.

How can I promote shared attention, and what part does it play in language development?

When a baby and their caregiver are focused on the same thing or activity, it's called joint attention. Engage in interactive tasks that demand shared attention and engagement to promote joint attention, such as naming and pointing out attractive objects.

What should I do if my infant exhibits delays in language development or appears insensitive to verbal cues?

Talk to your paediatrician if you have any worries regarding your baby's language development. Early intervention programs and speech therapy services are available for infants requiring further assistance to improve their communicative abilities.

How can I help my baby's language development at home by creating a language-rich environment?

Talk to your infant often, read aloud, sing, and play music to provide them with language-rich stimuli. Give your baby opportunities to converse with you and other caregivers by labelling items and behaviours in their surroundings.

In a multilingual household, should I be concerned if my kid babbles more in one language than the other?

Babies raised in bilingual households will likely prefer one language over another, depending on their developmental stage. They will probably become proficient in both languages over time if they are exposed to both regularly.

What indicators indicate my infant is starting to pick up words and basic commands?

When your baby responds to their name, looks toward familiar items when called upon, and obeys fundamental orders like "come here" or "give me the toy," these are indications that they are beginning to grasp words and simple commands.

Chapter Three

Feeding and diet for babies' growth

What signals indicate that my child is prepared to begin eating solid food?

The capacity to sit up with assistance, a demonstrated interest in food, the absence of the tongue-thrust reflex, and improved swallowing coordination are all pointers that your baby is prepared for solid meals. See your paediatrician before starting solid foods.

When is the right time to give my infant solid foods?

When a baby shows signs of readiness around six months, such as sitting up with assistance, displaying an interest in food, and losing the tongue-thrust reflex, the American Academy of Pediatrics advises introducing solid meals. However, some babies might be prepared as early as four months, so talking to your paediatrician is essential.

During this phase, how often should I breastfeed or bottle-feed my child?

Breastfed infants nurse eight or twelve times daily, depending on their needs. Babies fed formula may eat four to six ounces every three to four hours. Pay attention to your baby's hunger cues and feed them as necessary.

What signals indicate that my child is prepared to begin eating solid food?

When children are ready for solid meals, they should sit up straight, have substantial head control, reach for food to indicate interest, and no longer use their tongues to drive food out of their mouths.

Which foods are suitable to introduce to my infant first?

Start with simple one-ingredient purees of readily digested foods, including mashed avocado, boiled sweet potatoes, pureed bananas or pears, or iron-fortified rice cereal. One by one, gradually introduce new foods while checking for any indications of allergic reactions.

As my kids get closer to six months old, how can I ensure they get adequate nutrients from me?

Breast milk remains a baby's main nutritional supply for up to six months. For a good supply of milk, ensure you eat a nourished diet and drink lots of water. Demand-feeding will adapt to your baby's changing requirements.

What should I do if my infant refuses to consume solid foods or appears uninterested?

Babies often need some time to become used to new flavours and textures. Be patient. Give them little portions of food at a time, and if they refuse, try again later. Continue to offer breast milk or formula for nutrients and avoid forcing feedings.

When introducing solid foods to my kid, should I be concerned if they have a strong gag reflex?

Babies' innate gagging response helps keep them from choking. Babies frequently gag when they first start eating solid foods. Provide foods in bite-sized, soft, and easily handled portions to reduce the chance of choking.

How can I determine whether my child receives enough formula or breast milk?

Stable weight increase, satisfaction following feedings, multiple wet diapers per day, and reaching developmental milestones indicate that your baby is receiving adequate nourishment. If you are worried about your baby's feeding habits, speak with your paediatrician.

When should my infant start eating water?

Around six months of age, whether your baby is formula-fed or you live in a hot climate, you can start introducing water to their diet. Give little sips of boiling, cooled water in a cup; however, do not give water before six months of age since this may hinder the absorption of nutrients.

How can I wean my infant off of formula or breast milk to take solid foods?

Offer modest portions of mashed or pureed food once daily, then work up to two or three meals. Until your baby is completely weaned off of solid meals, continue to offer breast milk or formula along with them.

How can I determine when my child can move on to foods with thicker textures and greater complexity?

When your baby can sit up without much assistance, have the motor skills to move food to the back of their mouth without gagging, and express curiosity in different textures, they are ready for thicker and more complicated foods.

How can I see that my baby gets sufficient iron in their diet, and what part does iron play in it?

Iron is essential for your infant's general health and brain development. Iron-rich foods like pureed meats or fortified cereals may be necessary for breastfed babies to get extra iron. Even though formula provides enough iron for babies, when solid meals are given, they may still benefit from eating foods high in iron.

How can I give my baby allergy-friendly meals in a safe way?

One at a time, in tiny portions, introduce allergic foods, then wait a few days before introducing the next new food. Foods like peanuts, eggs, dairy, soy, wheat, fish, and shellfish are frequently allergic. Keep an eye out for any symptoms of allergic reactions, such as breathing difficulties, vomiting, hives, or rash.

If my infant is having trouble sucking or latching on when I'm nursing, what should I do?

If your infant has trouble sucking or latching, get assistance from a healthcare professional or lactation consultant. They can check for conditions like tongue knots or improper placement and offer advice on increasing breastfeeding success.

How can I ensure my infant drinks enough water, particularly in the summer?

Give your baby breast milk, formula, or small amounts of boiled, cooled water throughout the day, especially if it's hot outside or they look thirsty. Watch out for symptoms of dehydration, such as dry lips, dark urine, or irritability.

Which indicators point to my kid being prepared to move to a cup?

When your baby can sit up independently without assistance, try to grasp things and use coordi. Start with a sippy cup with a soft spout and handles.

What are some safe finger food options for my baby, and when should I start introducing them to them?

You can introduce soft, easy-to-grasp finger foods when your baby has developed the pincer grasp, which should happen around six. Safe choices include modest portions of well-cooked pasta, soft fruits like banana or avocado slices, and cooked veggies like broccoli florets or carrot sticks.

Should I be worried about intolerance?

You should speak with your paediatrician if your child has a food allergy or intolerance. If necessary, they can suggest diagnostic testing, assist in locating possible triggers, and offer advice on controlling your baby's food to prevent allergic responses.

What should I do if my child exhibits fussy eating habits or refuses to eat particular foods?

Infants are less likely than older children to exhibit picky eating practices. If your infant rejects some meals, keep giving them to them in moderation and experiment with other flavours or textures. Steer clear of force and pressure, and set an example for healthy eating habits.

How can I ensure my infant gets a balanced, diverse diet to suit their nutritional needs?

Present an assortment of nutrient-dense foods spanning multiple dietary categories, such as fruits, vegetables, grains, dairy or dairy substitutes, and protein sources like meat, chicken, fish, beans, and lentils. Your goal should be a hygienic diet with the necessary nutrients for development and growth.

Chapter Four

Nursing a baby through the half-year

When will my infant begin to spend the entire night asleep?

Around three to six months, many newborns commence sleep through the night for extended periods. Sleeping for longer lengths of time at night can be facilitated by creating a regular bedtime routine and encouraging healthy sleeping habits.

At this age, how much sleep does my kid need?

Between the ages of two and six months, babies generally require 14 to 16 hours of sleep per day, including naps during the day and overnight sleep. Individual sleep needs, however, can differ, and babies may sleep more or less than usual.

What kind of sleep schedule do babies in this age range usually follow?

During this time, babies can still be developing a regular sleep cycle. They may start to integrate nocturnal sleep into lengthier periods, typically with one- or two-night feedings, and take shorter naps throughout the day, lasting anywhere from thirty minutes to two hours.

How do I get my infant into a sleep routine?

Your child will be more likely to sleep if you establish a regular bedtime routine. A soothing bath, a light massage, reading a bedtime story, and lowering the lights to create a peaceful atmosphere are a few examples of activities that can be included in a sleep ritual.

If my baby is having trouble falling or staying asleep, what should I do?

If your infant has trouble falling asleep, try to create a regular bedtime ritual and sleeping space. Make sure the space is silent, dark, and comfortably chilled. If your infant awakens during the night, give them comfort and assurance, but steer clear of stimulating activities that could cause them to fall back asleep.

At what age should I start putting my infant to sleep, and what techniques may I employ?

Since newborns at this age can better self-soothe and manage their sleep patterns, most experts advise delaying sleep training until after six months. The Ferber, Weissbluth, and chair methods are popular sleep training techniques; nevertheless, selecting a strategy that complements your parenting style and your baby's temperament is critical.

Is it typical for my infant to wake up a lot at night at this point?

Yes, it's common for babies to wake up a lot during the night, particularly if they're breastfeeding or experiencing developmental milestones like growth spurts. Your kid may eventually begin to sleep through the night for extended periods as they age.

How can I help my infant take better naps during the day?

A regular sleep pattern and nap schedule can promote more restful daytime naps. If your baby seems sleepy, such as wiping their eyes or yawning, lay them down for a nap before they get too exhausted. Provide a peaceful, dark room that is suitable for sleeping in.

What are some telltale signals that my child is prepared to switch to a different sleep schedule or fewer naps?

Longer sleep and resistance to or skipping some naps are indicators that your baby might be ready to move to a different nap schedule or fewer naps. Observe your infant's sleeping habits and modify their nap schedule following instructions.

Should I be worried if my kid struggles to establish a schedule or has erratic sleep habits?

Babies frequently experience erratic sleep patterns, particularly during growth spurts or other developmental milestones. To rule out any underlying problems, speak with your paediatrician if your child routinely struggles to settle into a pattern or exhibits symptoms of sleep difficulties.

How can I help my infant develop sound sleeping habits over time?

Establishing a regular bedtime routine, making your home sleep-friendly, attending to your baby's sleep cues quickly, and fostering self-soothing abilities are vital in promoting healthy sleep habits. Your infant can develop healthy sleep habits if you are consistent and patient with them.

How can I tell my infant the difference between sleep throughout the day and night?

Encourage your baby to develop a regular sleep schedule by providing ample natural light during daytime feedings and interactions. In contrast, interaction and feedings during the night should be peaceful, quiet, and darkly lighted. To promote longer sleep cycles

Does my baby's sleep regression during this period seem normal?

Yes, sleep regressions are frequent in babies, starting at four months of age and continuing through other developmental milestones. Your baby's sleep patterns may be momentarily disturbed by these regressions, but they are usually independent with patience and consistency.

What methods may I use to lull my baby to sleep without using food or rocking?

Establish a regular bedtime routine and put your baby to sleep, awake but drowsy, to encourage self-soothing. Don't create sleep associations that on feeding or rocking your child to sleep;

How can I assist my infant sleep soundly so that the chance of SIDS is decreased?

Adhere to the safe sleep guidelines recommended by establishments like the American Academy of Pediatrics (AAP). These strategies include putting your baby to sleep on their back, using a flat, firm surface, avoiding stuffed animals and soft bedding in the crib, and keeping the area where they sleep free of hazards.

What should I do if my infant has trouble falling back asleep or wakes up often at night?

If your infant wakes up often at night, identify the underlying reason(s), such as hunger, discomfort, or sleep associations. Take care of urgent requirements, such as changing diapers or feeding, and provide comfort without contributing to unfavourable sleep associations.

How can I assist my kid in switching from sharing a bed or co-sleeping to sleeping in a crib or cot of their own?

Beginning with naps in the crib or bassinet, gradually increase the time your baby sleeps in their room at night. Establish a secure and cosy sleeping space and provide comforting items like a blanket or plush animal to reassure the sleeper.

What are some telltale indicators that my child is too or too tired?

Overtiredness manifests as fussiness, eye rubbing, yawning, and trouble falling asleep. Short naps, frequent awakenings, and trouble falling asleep can all be indicators of under-tiredness. Adapt your baby's routine and sleep schedule to suit their unique requirements and indications.

How can I help my baby learn to comfort themselves and go back to sleep alone at night?

Giving your infant the freedom to sleep independently at night will help them develop self-soothing abilities. When your baby needs comfort or assurance, provide it, but as time goes on, lessen your interventions so they can learn to soothe themselves and go back to sleep.

Should I be concerned if my child has issues falling asleep at night or wakes up often?

While some nighttime awakenings occur daily in infants, more frequent or longer ones may point to a more severe problem, such as discomfort, hunger, or sleep problems. Monitor your infant's sleeping habits and speak with your paediatrician if you have any worries.

How can I meet my baby's sleep demands while prioritizing my relaxation and well-being as a parent?
Make self-care a priority by asking your spouse, family, or friends for help splitting the caregiving duties. To refuel and preserve your well-being, prioritize restorative activities, pause when necessary, and engage in relaxing practices.

Chapter Five

Monitoring your baby's emotional and social growth

During this phase, how can I support my infant's social development?

Playing face-to-face with your infant, grinning, maintaining eye contact, and attending to their cues for involvement and attention will all help foster social interactions. Promote social contact between caregivers and family members.

How can I encourage attachment and bonding with my baby during this phase?

When you provide your infant with responsive care—cuddles, comforts, eye contact, and verbal interactions—they bond and become attached. To strengthen your relationship, spend quality time with your infant, pay attention to their cues, and show them lots of physical affection.

When will my child begin to smile and react to social cues?

Babies usually begin to smile socially around two to three months of age and react to their caretakers' voices and facial expressions. They could also start to coo and make vocalizations to socialize with others.

What are some indicators that my child is becoming interested in other people and social awareness?

Making eye contact, turning to face familiar sounds, reaching out for comfort or a handshake, and displaying an interest in people and social interactions are all indications of social awareness. Additionally, your infant can begin to express preferences for particular caretakers or acquaintances.

How can I use play to support my infant's social development?

Take part in face-to-face interactive play activities with your infant, such as talking, smiling, and making silly noises. Use objects that promote social contact, like mirrors, rattles, and plush animals, with different textures and colours.

How can I encourage shared attention in my kid, and what part does it play in their social development?

The term "joint attention" describes how your infant and another person share concentration on a thing or activity. By naming and pointing out fascinating objects, you can promote joint attention. You can also follow your baby's lead and explore the environment together.

Is it typical for my infant to exhibit separation or stranger anxiety at this age?

Yes, as babies grow more conscious of their caretakers and their environment, it is typical for them to exhibit symptoms of separation anxiety and anxiety from strangers. Around six or eight months of age is usually when these fears peak, and as your infant grows more accustomed to people and routines, they progressively go away.

How can I make my infant feel safe and at ease around strangers?

By gently introducing new people and situations to your infant and giving them lots of warmth and confidence, you may help them feel secure. When interacting with others, stay close to your child and let them come to you and new people at their own pace.

What are some indicators that my child is growing in empathy and emotional intelligence?

Empathy manifests as mirrored facial expressions or movements in response to other people's emotions, bringing consolation to a weeping caregiver or sibling, and expressing concern or distress in response to another person's distress.

How can I assist my infant in developing emotionally and in learning how to control their emotions?

When your infant is distressed, soothe and reassure them; validate their feelings by naming and recognizing them. Establish a soothing and supportive atmosphere while setting an example of healthy coping mechanisms for handling emotions.

When should I start to worry about my child's social and emotional growth?

Although every baby grows at their rate, you should speak with your paediatrician if you observe any notable social or emotional developmental delays or regressions in your child, such as prolonged withdrawal, excessive fussiness, or trouble interacting with others.

How can I help my infant develop secure bonding and connection at this phase?

Respondent caregiving, which includes quickly attending to your baby's demands for feeding, comfort, and emotional support, fosters attachment and bonding. Building trust and a strong attachment link with your baby is facilitated by attentively attending to their cues, such as crying or reaching out.

What are some significant ways I can interact with my infant to help their social development?

Make eye contact, smile, and speak to your kid in a soothing voice when interacting with them face-to-face. To promote back-and-forth conversation, enthusiastically react to their coos and babble and imitate their noises.

What telltale indications should I watch out for as my baby's social awareness develops during this stage?

Social awareness increases as your kid grows more perceptive of the people and surroundings around them. Familiar voices should be turned toward; faces should be followed with the gaze, and smiling, gesturing, or reaching out are indications of social awareness.

Is it typical for my infant to feel more at ease among new people when they are with familiar caretakers rather than strangers?

It is common for babies to exhibit a preference for known caretakers and to feel anxious about strangers when they are between six and eight months old. Introduce new people to your baby gently, calmly, and reassuringly. Let your infant watch from a distance before interacting with them to help them feel more at ease.

How can I support my baby's exploration and playtime to help them develop their social skills?

Your infant has a vital opportunity to explore their surroundings and engage with people and items during playtime. To promote communication and social interaction abilities, engage in interactive play activities like peekaboo, gentle tickling, and toy passing back and forth.

How can I encourage my child's emotional growth and teach them to control their emotions?

Validating your baby's emotions and supporting responsive care for their emotional development. When your baby is angry, comfort and reassure them; by creating a safe and nurturing atmosphere, you can also help them learn to soothe themselves. Exhibit appropriate emotional expression and coping mechanisms.

What are some indicators that my child is growing in empathy and emotional intelligence?

Offering consolation to a weeping caretaker or sister, exhibiting mirrored facial expressions or gestures in reaction to others' feelings, and expressing worry or distress in response to another person's distress are examples of demonstrating empathy.

If my infant exhibits symptoms of separation anxiety at this time, should I be concerned?

Your infant will naturally experience some level of separation anxiety during this phase as they grow closer to dependable caretakers. However, seek advice and assistance from your paediatrician if your child's separation anxiety becomes severe or lasts longer than anticipated throughout their developmental stage.

How can I foster a positive feeling of confidence and self-worth in my child?

Create a loving, caring environment for your infant to feel accepted, appreciated, and respected. Give them lots of credit and support for their efforts and successes and chances for independence and self-discovery within secure bounds.

How can I ensure that their social and emotional growth does not stop when my child gets older?

Maintain your attentive and compassionate caregiving, participate in deep conversations, and allow chances for discovery and socialization. Keep an eye on your child's growth, acknowledge their accomplishments, and consult medical specialists if you worry about their emotional or social welfare.

Chapter Six

The process of teething and its impact on baby development

How can I support my infant while they are teething?

Give your child cold teething rings or teething toys to help relieve painful gums. Apply a hygienic finger to massage your baby's gums, or give them a clean, wet washcloth to chew on.

What are the telltale indicators of baby teething, and when does it usually begin?

Although it might vary, babies usually begin teething between 4 and 6 months. Increased drooling, swollen or sensitive gums, fussiness or irritability, gnawing on objects, and disturbed sleep are some of the symptoms associated with teething.

How can I ease my baby's discomfort during teething?

Give your infant cold teething rings or toys to nibble on; the pressure will assist in reducing gum irritation. A damp gauze pad or clean fingertips can gently massage the gums. Before taking any drugs or teething gels, speak with your paediatrician.

What are some safe and efficient home remedies for teething I may try?

Give your baby cold, soft meals like yoghurt or pureed fruit to relieve painful gums. Another option is to give your infant a fresh, moist washcloth to touch or gnaw on their gums. Amber teething jewellery and necklaces should be avoided since they can choke a child.

Is my baby's heightened fussiness and irritability during teething normal?

Indeed, increased fussiness or irritability is typical because of the discomfort and soreness in the gums during teething. Keeping your infant comfortable and providing calming remedies will help ease their pain.

What is the average duration of teething, and when can I anticipate teeth erupting?

While it can differ from newborn to baby, teething takes several months. Teeth can erupt as early as 4 to 6 months of age, with the upper front teeth (upper central incisors) typically emerging first and the lower front teeth (lower central incisors) coming second.

What should I do if my baby's discomfort from teething is keeping them from sleeping?

Provide consolation and assurance to your infant when teething discomfort causes them to wake up during the night. Gum pain can be reduced using calming methods like soft rocking, snuggling, teething toys, or cold teethers. Stick to a regular bedtime schedule to assist your infant in unwinding and returning to sleep.

Is it cause for concern if my infant has a low-grade fever when teething?

While low-grade fevers (below 38°C, or 100.4°F) are often linked to teething, they usually don't warrant alarm. If your paediatrician recommends it, keep an eye on your baby's temperature and give them comfort measures like cool compresses or the proper amount of infant acetaminophen.

How can I tell the difference between signs of an illness and teething symptoms?

Drooling, becoming irritable, and gnawing on things are common symptoms of teething. To rule out disease or infection, speak with your paediatrician if your baby exhibits symptoms such as high fever, diarrhoea, or excessive fussiness that are not typical of teething.

Can my baby's eating habits or appetite alter due to teething?

Yes, your baby's hunger and eating habits may be momentarily impacted by teething discomfort. To help your infant keep hydrated and nourished during teething episodes, offer soft, easy-to-eat meals and nurse or bottle-feed frequently.

How can I reassure and soothe my kids when they are going through teething?

Give your baby lots of warm embraces, kisses, and comforting words to help them through the discomfort of teething. To assist in calming and soothing them, gently rock or use rhythmic motions. You can also help relieve stress and anxiety by keeping your surroundings peaceful.

In the case of discomfort in the gums, what are indications that my kid is teething?

You can have more irritation, altered sleep patterns, excessive drooling, a mild rash around the mouth, and a propensity to chew on fingers or objects, in addition to gum soreness.

For teething discomfort, should I give my kid over-the-counter pain relievers? If yes, how much should I give?

It would be best if you spoke with your paediatrician before giving your child any medication, even over-the-counter analgesics. If your baby's paediatrician advises it, carefully follow their directions and use the recommended dosage for your baby's weight and age.

Is there a natural way to make my infant feel less uncomfortable while teething?

Some parents discover that giving their child a clean, chilled washcloth to gnaw on, some chilled teething toys, or a gentle finger massage might help relieve their gum pain. You can also try serving cold meals like yoghurt or applesauce for calming relief.

My infant seems to be teething and drooling a lot. How can I deal with this, and is it normal?

Yes, one of the most typical signs of teething is increased drooling. Use absorbent bibs to dry your baby's chin and chest when they drool excessively. To prevent skin irritation, use a barrier cream and a soft towel to wipe up drool gently.

Which safe teething toys are suitable for my baby to gnaw on?

Seek for teething toys composed of safe materials like natural rubber or silicone that are free of BPA. Some standard options are silicone teethers shaped like fruits or animals, textured teethers, and teething rings. Teething toys should be cleaned and inspected for wear or damage regularly.

Is it possible for my kid to get a diaper rash or diarrhoea from teething?

Teething does not usually result in diarrhoea or diaper rash, but because it increases saliva production, some babies may have altered bowel movements or moderate diaper rash. Practice good diaper care and use diaper creams to protect the skin.

It appears that my baby's teething is interfering with their sleep. How can I improve their quality of sleep?

Provide consolation and assurance to your infant when teething discomfort causes them to wake up during the night. Consider making pleasant changes to your baby's sleeping environment, including playing white noise to help you rest or using a cool-mist humidifier.

Can my infant get a runny nose or cough from teething?

Coughing and runny noses are not symptoms of teething; however, some babies may experience moderate congestion due to increased drooling during this time. Apply a bulb syringe or nasal aspirator to clear your baby's nasal passages. If symptoms worsen or continue, speak with your paediatrician.

If my infant won't eat or drink because they are having teething pain, should I worry?

While it's normal for babies to experience changes in their appetite or feeding habits throughout the teething process, it's crucial to make sure your child continues to receive food and fluids. To avoid dehydration, provide soft, manageable foods and promote frequent breastfeeding or bottle-feeding.

When will my baby's teeth erupt entirely, and how long does teething discomfort usually last?

The discomfort associated with teething can vary in length and severity, but it usually lasts a few days to weeks until each tooth erupts through the gums. By six to ten months, most babies will have their first teeth, the lower central incisors, and progressively more teeth will erupt.

Can a fever in my infant be caused by teething?

Although some parents believe that low-grade fevers are caused by teething, there isn't much scientific data to back up this theory. Fevers higher than 100.4°F (38°C) are usually not brought on by teething. Should your infant's fever exceed this threshold, it can result from an unrelated ailment, and you ought to speak with a healthcare provider.

It appears like my infant is biting while she breastfeeds. Is teething a factor in this?

Indeed, some newborns bite during nursing as they become used to the feel of their new teeth. But biting during nursing can sometimes indicate other problems, like an incorrect latch or pain. Give your infant a firm but gentle "no biting" cue and gently remove them from the breast if they bite while breastfeeding.

How do I get my infant to sleep through the teething process comfortably?

Establish a comfortable sleeping environment for your infant by using soft, breathable bedding, keeping the room at a suitable temperature, and giving them the proper support with a firm mattress. Give your baby calming practices before bedtime, including soft rocking, hugging, or a warm bath.

Teething seems to have reddened and flushed my baby's cheeks. Is this typical?

Some babies may have flushed cheeks because of the enlarged blood flow to the gums during teething. While flushed or red cheeks often indicate that your baby is teething, keep an eye on their general health and behaviour to be sure there aren't any other symptoms of disease or pain.

Can my kid get earache or start pulling their ears during teething?

While ear discomfort is not directly caused by teething, some babies may feel pain in their ears due to teething. Make sure there are no other possible reasons for your baby's ear pain or pulling at their ears, and if needed, get advice from your paediatrician.

How do I stop drooling so much when I am teething?

Frequently wipe your baby's chin and chest with a clean towel or bib to control excessive drooling. Moreover, a soft, absorbent bib can keep clothes dry and minimize irritation. Change wet bibs and clothes to prevent skin irritation as soon as possible.

Should I feed my infant cookies or biscuits to gnaw on while they are teething?

Babies should not be given biscuits or cookies while teething because they can be choking hazards and may have additional sugars or preservatives. To assist in relieving painful gums, substitute safe teething toys or cold teething rings.

How can I ease my baby's teething discomfort when we go on trips or other events?

When travelling or going on an expedition, give your baby some respite by including a teething toy or cold teething ring in your diaper bag. Carry a fresh cloth or bib to wipe away saliva and offer comfort measures like soft rocking or hugging as required.

Is my baby's increased neediness or clinginess during teething normal?

Indeed, it is typical for infants to turn to their caretakers for additional consolation and assurance during teething periods. Throughout this challenging period, give your baby lots of hugs, cuddles, and comforting words to help them feel safe and cherished.

When should I take my infant to a doctor if they have trouble teething?

Even though teething pain is a typical and often benign aspect of infancy, you should see a doctor if your baby's symptoms are severe, ongoing, or present, together with other unsettling symptoms like diarrhoea, a high temperature, or a refusal to eat or drink.

Chapter Seven

Maternal and child health

What are some strategies for helping my baby and me develop a healthy attachment?

Foster a healthy connection by attending to your infant's needs as soon as possible, providing consolation and assurance, and participating in loving activities like rocking, snuggling, and gentle play. To foster bonding, engage in skin-to-skin contact and babywearing.

When is the best time to book my child's next well-child visit?

Most paediatricians advise planning well-child visits for immunizations, developmental tests, and routine exams at 2, 4, and 6 months. Make an appointment with your child's paediatrician's office for your child's upcoming examination.

Which vaccines are safe for my kid to receive between two and six months?

Immunizations against pneumococcal disease (PCV13), rotavirus, diphtheria, tetanus, pertussis (DTaP), polio (IPV), and Haemophilus influenzae type b (Hib) are commonly advised for newborns between the ages of two and six months. These immunizations are necessary to safeguard your child's health and are considered safe.

It looks like my baby has a cold. How can I help them feel better?

When your baby gets a cold, you may help them feel better by giving them breast milk or formula to stay hydrated, using a cool mist humidifier to reduce congestion, and using a bulb syringe or nasal aspirator to pressure their nasal passages gently. Don't give infants over-the-counter cold remedies without first talking to your paediatrician.

How should I respond if my child has a fever?

When your baby's temperature rises above 100.4°F (38°C), carefully note it and contact your paediatrician for advice. Provide comfort measures, including ensuring your baby drinks enough water, putting them in light clothing, and giving them medication to lower their fever if your paediatrician advises.

The skin on my newborn seems flaky and dry. How can I assist in hydrating their skin?

Use a light, fragrance-free moisturizing lotion or cream on your baby's dry skin after baths and as needed during the day. Choose products designed especially for baby skin instead of ones with solid chemicals or smells.

How should I respond if my child has diaper rash?

If your infant has a diaper rash, change their diapers regularly and let their skin air dry in between to keep the area clean and dry. Use a thick barrier ointment or lotion to shield the skin and aid healing. Speak with your paediatrician if the rash doesn't go away or gets worse.

How can I prevent my baby from receiving diaper rash?
Replace your baby's diaper immediately after every bowel movement and several times daily to prevent diaper rash. It would be best to refrain from using harsh soaps or wipes that could irritate their skin. Before changing your baby's diaper, let their skin air dry and apply a thick barrier cream or ointment to keep them safe from wetness and irritation.

If my kid spits up a lot after feedings, what should I do?
It's probably just regular reflux if your infant spits up a lot after feedings but is otherwise healthy and growing weight. Try feeding your baby upright, giving them frequent burps throughout feedings, and refraining from overfeeding to reduce the likelihood of them spitting up. Speak with your paediatrician if the throwing up is severe or occurs with other symptoms.

I think my infant is constipated. How can I assist in easing their constipation?

In addition to providing plenty of breast milk or formula to keep your baby hydrated, you should incorporate fibre-rich meals like pureed fruits and vegetables into their diet if they have started solid foods to treat constipation. To help encourage bowel motions, try cycling leg movements and gently massaging your baby's abdomen. Speak with your paediatrician if constipation doesn't go away.

When should I take my baby to the doctor if there are health concerns?

If your child exhibits indications of an illness, such as a high temperature, breathing difficulties, frequent vomiting or diarrhoea, lethargy or excessive sleepiness, unwillingness to eat or drink, dehydration, or other worrisome symptoms, have them checked out by a doctor. As a parent, if you have any worries about your baby's health, follow your instincts and speak with your paediatrician.

My baby looks like a grumpy person. Can you tell whether this is colic and how to treat it?

Excessive crying or fussiness in an otherwise healthy newborn is a sign of colic. Try soothing methods like pacifiers, white noise, soft rocking, and swaddling to help control colic. For further assessment and advice, speak with your paediatrician about whether your child's colic is severe or continuing.

Does my baby's irregular bowel movements seem normal?

Yes, irregular bowel motions are usual, especially if a baby is breastfed. While formula-fed newborns may have fewer but larger bowel movements each day, breastfed babies may have multiple bowel movements daily. Generally, irregularity in your baby's faeces is not a reason for concern as long as they are soft and pass easily.

It looks like my infant is tugging at their ears. Can it be an infection in the ears?

Pulling on the ears may occasionally be a sign of an ear infection, particularly if it is coupled with other symptoms like fever, fussiness, or trouble falling asleep. See your paediatrician for an evaluation and the best course of action if you think your child may have an ear infection.

How can I clean my baby's ears safely?

During your baby's bath, gently clean the outer ear with a damp washcloth. Nothing, not even cotton swabs, should be put into your baby's ear canal as this could injure them or push wax farther within the ear. See your paediatrician if you observe any significant wax buildup or have any concerns regarding your baby's ears.

The stump of my baby's umbilical cord hasn't come off yet. Do I need to worry?

The stump of the umbilical cord often stays attached for a few weeks before coming off by itself. Refrain from concealing the area with tight clothes or diapers, and keep it dry and clean. See your paediatrician for any infection-related symptoms, such as redness, swelling, or discharge.

My baby's skin has turned red. How do I identify the problem and the best course of action?

Various things, such as skin irritants, allergic reactions, or diaper rash, may cause a rash. Closely inspect the rash and consider any dietary, skincare, or environmental changes that may have occurred recently. For a precise diagnosis and treatment plan, speak with your physician if the rash disappears or worsens.

How can I protect my kid from sunburn and heat-related illnesses in hot weather?

Breast milk or formula should be given often, and your infant should be dressed in lightweight, breathable clothing to stay well-hydrated. Reduce your child's exposure to the sun, especially in the afternoon and evening, and protect exposed skin areas with a broad-spectrum sunscreen for young children. In periods of intense heat, seek cover indoors or shade.

It appears like my infant has a cough. When should I get medical help, and what could be the cause?

Many things, such as common colds, respiratory infections, allergies, or irritants, can induce coughing in babies. Keep a close eye on your baby's cough; if it gets worse, lasts longer, or is accompanied by other worrisome symptoms like fever, breathing difficulties, or wheezing, get medical help.

When is the right time to start giving my kid solid foods, and how can I do it safely?

After your baby reaches the age of six months, or when they begin to exhibit signs of readiness like sitting up with assistance and displaying an interest in food, gradually introduce solid foods into their diet. As your baby grows, start with simple, one-ingredient soft foods like pureed fruits or veggies and work your way up to more textured options.

What should I do if a new food triggers an allergic reaction in my baby?

Stop feeding your infant immediately and get medical help if they exhibit any signs of an allergic response, such as hives, lip or facial swelling, vomiting, or trouble breathing, following a new meal. Speak with your paediatrician for advice on managing your baby's allergies and avoiding trigger foods.

Chapter Eight

Common issues regarding infant development

It appears that my infant is suffering from separation anxiety. How can I make it easier for them to live without me?

Anxiety related to separation is a regular aspect of a baby's growth and usually appears at six months of age. Create dependable routines, provide comfort items like a cherished blanket or toy, and soothe them with reassuring words and gestures when you must be apart to help them cope.

There are specific periods of the day when my infant cries uncontrollably. Is this perhaps colic, and if so, how can I treat it?

In otherwise healthy babies, colic is characterized by protracted, intense sobbing bouts that usually begin about two weeks of age and end three to four months later. Try calming methods like swaddling, soft rocking, or a pacifier to help control colic. See your paediatrician if you need any further help or direction.

My infant is susceptible to loud noises and is easily startled. Is this typical, and if so, how can I reassure them?

Infants often have a startle reflex and are sensitive to loud noises; these traits eventually disappear as they age. Use calming, soft sounds, establish a quiet and predictable atmosphere, and gently reassure your baby when they make unusual noises or movements to help them feel safer.

My infant appears to be fussier and more agitated than usual. Is overstimulation the cause of this, and if so, how can I avoid it?

When a newborn is exposed to too much sensory information, overstimulation can happen, which increases fussiness or irritation. Provide a quiet and comforting environment, restrict your baby's exposure to bright lights or loud noises, and engage them in gentle, rhythmic activities to help them unwind and minimize overstimulation.

Compared to other babies their age, my baby doesn't seem to be meeting developmental milestones as quickly. Do I need to worry?

Since each infant develops at their own rate, there are frequently little differences in the developmental milestones they accomplish. But if you're worried about your child's growth, get an assessment and advice from your paediatrician.

One caregiver seemed to be preferred by my infant above others. Is this typical, and if so, how can I foster goodwill among other caregivers?

It is common for infants to express preferences for dependable caregivers, particularly for primary caregivers who offer comfort and attention regularly. To foster good connections with other caregivers, providing chances for quality time spent together and shared activities that encourage bonding is essential.

My infant now acts possessive or envious of me when I engage with other people or things. How can I politely confront this behaviour?

When your baby expresses jealousy or possessiveness, respond to them with compassion and understanding. Provide comfort and compassion to make them feel safe and cherished. To foster social skills and emotional growth, set an example of sharing and taking turns in your interactions.

It appears like my infant is having teething pain. How can I comfort and care for you sensitively at this time?

When your baby is uncomfortable with teething, give them a gentle massage, cold teething toys or rings to gnaw on, and use calming methods like rocking or cuddling to help them feel better. Be patient and understanding when responding to your baby's indications and wants.

My youngster has begun to exhibit symptoms of nervousness around strangers. What can I do to help them get through this stage?

Anxiety about strangers is a typical developmental stage that usually appears in infants between the ages of 6 and 8 months. To help your infant, gently and reassuringly introduce new people to them and offer consolation and assurance when they are around people they are not familiar with. Allow your infant to approach new settings at their speed and respect their need for familiarity.

My baby has trouble falling asleep or sticking to a bedtime schedule. How can I gently assist them in forming sound sleeping habits?

Create a regular sleep schedule that includes relaxing activities like a warm bath, a light massage, and quiet time before bed. Pay attention to their sleep cues to help your baby feel safe and at ease before bed and respond patiently and consistently. You can also provide comfort and reassurance when needed.

My infant seems to be spitting up after meals a lot or having reflux. How do I handle this delicately?

Try feeding your baby upright and frequently burping them during feedings to reduce air swallowing if they are having reflux or spitting up a lot. Don't immediately put your baby to sleep after feedings; instead, give smaller, more frequent feedings.

See your paediatrician if your reflux symptoms worsen or don't go away.

My infant has a rash on his diaper. How can I calm their itchy skin with delicate care?

By frequently changing diapers and letting your baby's skin air dry in between changes, you can help relieve diaper rash by keeping the region clean and dry. Use a thick barrier ointment or lotion to shield the skin and aid healing. Steer clear of solid chemicals and products containing alcohol, and use soft wipes without any scent.

Constipation or discomfort during bowel motions appears to bother my baby. How can I give them considerate attention that will make them feel better?

If your baby has begun solid food, give them gentle care to ease their discomfort during bowel movements or constipation by promoting hydration with plenty of fluids and introducing fibre-rich foods into their diet. To promote bowel motions, gently massage your baby's tummy and reward frequent movement.

It appears that my baby's skin is sensitive or irritated. How can I give their sensitive skin the attention it needs to be protected?

Use gentle skincare products without fragrances designed for infants to safeguard your baby's sensitive skin. Select supple, airy materials for clothing and bedding, and keep your child away from harsh chemicals or allergens that could aggravate skin sensitivity.

It looks like my baby is teething and is uncomfortable or fussy. How can I support them during this trying time with sensitive care?

Provide your baby with loving care to help them deal with the discomfort of teething by giving them cooled teething toys or rings to gnaw on, rocking or snuggling them, and employing other calming strategies. During this challenging stage, be patient and understanding when attending to your baby's demands.

My infant appears to be becoming sensitive to shifts in their schedule or surroundings. How can I give them considerate care so they can adjust?

When your baby's surroundings or routine changes, give them thoughtful care that tries to keep things as predictable and consistent as possible. During times of transition, provide consolation and assurance. To reduce tension and anxiety, enact changes gradually and soothingly.

It seems like my infant is sensitive or in discomfort when having their diaper changed. How can I give them delicate

attention to make changing their diapers more comfortable?

During diaper changes, care carefully by avoiding forceful rubbing or scouring of the skin and using gentle, fragrance-free wipes. To protect against moisture and irritation, apply a thick barrier cream or ointment. To assist your infant feel secure and at ease, use calming words and gestures.

It appears that my infant is sensitive to specific materials or textures. How can I give them delicate care that will guarantee their comfort?

To reduce irritability or pain, give your infant attentive care by dressing and sleeping in soft, breathable materials. When washing your baby's clothes, steer clear of items with sharp edges or tags that could irritate their skin. Also, use mild detergents without any strong chemicals or scents.

It seems like my baby is sensitive to bright lights or loud noises. How can I give them attentive care to make them feel comfortable?

Create a tranquil and comforting space for your infant with soft lighting and soothing noises to demonstrate sensitive care. Reduce your baby's exposure to bright lights and loud noises or unexpected sounds that could surprise or overwhelm them by using blackout curtains or shades.

It appears that my infant is sensitive to temperature changes. How can I give them delicate care to guarantee their comfort and well-being?

Dressing your baby in layers will help them stay warm without being too hot or too cold. It is delicate care. To keep your baby at a reasonable temperature for play and sleep, keep an eye on their comfort and make any necessary adjustments to their bedding or clothes.

About the Author

ADEGBOYE S. ADURAGBEMI is an African manager, business administrator, entrepreneur, and motivational speaker. ADEGBOYE has a BA from Yale University, an IPMA from Adonai University, and a Master's in Business Administration (MBA) from the University of Salford, Manchester.

He was born in South Africa but is presently based in Nigeria as a motivational speaker and marriage counsellor in institutions, sectors, and seminars with young and upcoming managers all over Africa.

Acknowledgements

I want to express my sincere gratitude to everyone who helped with the "FAQ on Communication in Marriage." Their encouragement, insight, and support have been priceless throughout this journey.

I want to start by acknowledging the fact that, without God, this guide wouldn't have been possibly achieved.

And also, to my spouse, who has always been motivating and supportive in making this task successful, I will always love and appreciate you.

I have many couples to appreciate who have shared their experiences, challenges, and victories with me over the years. Your openness, weakness, and tenacity have enhanced the book's pages and provided priceless insights into the difficulties of marriage communication.

My sincere gratitude goes to my family and friends for their continuous support and encouragement during this journey. Your wise advice, tolerance, and words of support have helped me get through the complicated process of writing and releasing this book.

I sincerely thank the specialists and experts who kindly offered their knowledge and skills in marriage and communication. Your advice and thoughts have improved this book's quality and depth, and I appreciate your contributions.

Finally, I would like to express my profound gratitude to all of the readers of this work. As you journey through the communication process in your marriage, I hope that the knowledge, direction, and encouragement provided within these pages will inspire and empower you.

I sincerely appreciate your help.

www.ingramcontent.com/pod-product-compliance
Lightning Source LLC
Chambersburg PA
CBHW040159160726
48006CB00014B/1815